Adobe Premiere Pro CC Keyboard Shortcuts

By

U. C-Abel Books.

All Rights Reserved

First Edition: 2017

ISBN-13: 978-1543227901
ISBN-10: 1543227902

Published by U. C-Abel Books.

Table of Contents

Acknowledgement.

All thanks to God Almighty for enabling us to bring this work to this point. He is a wonder indeed.

We want to specially appreciate the great company, Adobe Systems Inc. for their hard work and style of reasoning in providing the public with helpful programs and resources, and for helping us with some of the tips and keyboard shortcuts included in this book.

Dedication

The dedication of this title goes to users of Adobe Premiere Pro CC all over the world.

How We Began.

We enjoy using shortcuts because they set us on a high plane that astonishes people around us when we work with them. As wonderful shortcuts users, the worst eyesore we witness in computer operation is to see somebody sluggishly struggling to execute a task through mouse usage when in actual sense shortcuts will help to save that person time. Most people have asked us to help them with a list of keyboard shortcuts that can make them work as smartly as we do and that drove us into research to broaden our knowledge and truly help them as they demanded, that is the reason for the existence of this book. It is a great tool for lovers of shortcuts, and those who want to join the group.

Most times the things we love don't come by easily. It is our love for keyboard shortcuts that made us to bear long sleepless nights like owls just to make sure we get the best out of it, and it is the best we got that we are sharing with you in this book. You cannot be the same at computing after reading this book. The time you entrusted to our care is an expensive possession and we promise not to mess it up.

Thank you.

What to Know Before You Begin.

General Notes.

1. Most of the keyboard shortcuts you will see in this book refer to the U.S. keyboard layout. Keys for other layouts might not correspond exactly to the keys on a U.S. keyboard. Keyboard shortcuts for laptop computers might also differ.

2. It is important to note that when using shortcuts to perform any command, you should make sure the target area is active, if not, you may get a wrong result. Example, if you want to highlight all texts you must make sure the text field is active and if an object, make sure the object area is active. The active area is always known by the location where the cursor of your computer blinks.

3. On a Mac keyboard, the Command key is denoted with the ⌘symbol.

4. If a function key doesn't work on your Mac as you expect it to, press the Fn key in addition to the function key. If you don't want to press the Fn key every time, you can change your Apple system preferences.

5. The plus (+) sign that comes in the middle of keyboard shortcuts simply means the keys are

meant to be combined or held down together not to be added as one of the shortcut keys. In a case where plus sign is needed; it will be duplicated (++).

6. Many keyboards assign special functions to function keys, by default. To use the function key for other purposes, you have to press Fn+the function key.

7. For keyboard shortcuts in which you press one key immediately followed by another key, the keys are separated by a comma (,).

8. For chapters that have more than one topic, search for "A fresh topic" to see the beginning of a topic, and "End of Topic" to see the end of a topic.

9. It is also important to note that the keyboard shortcuts, tips, and techniques listed in this book are for users of Adobe Premiere Pro CC.

10. To get more information on this title visit ucabelbooks.wordpress.com and search the site using keywords related to it.

11. Our chief website is under construction.

Some Short Forms You Will Find in This Book and Their Full Meaning.

Here are short forms used in this Adobe Premiere Pro CC Keyboard Shortcuts book and their full meaning.

1. Win - Windows logo key
2. Tab - Tabulate Key
3. Shft - Shift Key
4. Prt sc - Print Screen
5. Num Lock - Number Lock Key
6. F - Function Key
7. Esc - Escape Key
8. Ctrl - Control Key
9. Caps Lock - Caps Lock Key
10. Alt - Alternate Key

CHAPTER 1.

Fundamental Knowledge of Keyboard Shortcuts.

Without the existence of the keyboard, there wouldn't have been anything like keyboard shortcuts so in this chapter we will learn a little about the computer keyboard before moving to keyboard shortcuts.

1. Definition of Computer Keyboard.

This is an input device that is used to send data to computer memory.

Sketch of a Keyboard

1.1 Types of Keyboard.

i. Standard (Basic) Keyboard.
ii. Enhanced (Extended) Keyboard.

i. **Standard Keyboard:** This is a keyboard designed during the 1800s for mechanical typewriters with just 10 function keys (F keys) placed at the left side of it.

ii. **Enhanced Keyboard:** This is the current 101 to 102-key keyboard that is included in almost all the personal computers (PCs) of nowadays, which has 12 function keys, usually at the top side of it.

1.2 Segments of the keyboard

- Numeric keys.
- Alphabetic keys.
- Punctuation keys.
- Windows Logo key.
- Function keys.
- Special keys.

Numeric Keys: Numeric keys are keys with numbers from **0 - 9**.

Alphabetic Keys: These are keys that have alphabets on them, ranging from **A** to **Z**.

Punctuation Keys: These are keys of the keyboard used for punctuation, examples include comma, full stop, colon, question marks, hyphen, etc.

Windows Logo Key: A key on Microsoft Computer keyboard with its logo displayed on it. Search for this ⊞ on your keyboard.

Apple Key: This also known as Command key is a modifier key that you can find on an Apple keyboard. It usually has the image of an apple or command logo on it. Search for this on your Apple keyboard ⌘

Function Keys: These are keys that have **F** on them which are usually combined with other keys. They are F1 - F12, and are also in the class called *Special Keys*.

Special Keys: These are keys that perform special functions. They include: Tab, Ctrl, Caps lock, Insert, Prt sc, alt gr, Shift, Home, Num lock, Esc, and many others. Special keys differ according to the type of computer involved. In some keyboard layout, especially laptops, the keys that turn the speaker on/off, the one that increases/decreases volume, the key that turns the computer Wifi on/off are also special keys.

Other Special Keys Worthy of Note.

Enter Key: This is located at the right-hand corner of most keyboards. It is used to send messages to the computer to execute commands, in most cases it is used to mean "Ok" or "Go".

Escape Key (ESC): This is the first key on the upper left of most keyboards. It is used to cancel routines, close menus and select options such as **Save** according to circumstances.

Control Key (CTRL): It is located on the bottom row of the left and right hand side of the keyboard. They also work with the function keys to execute commands using Keyboard shortcuts (key combinations).

Alternate Key (ALT): It is located on the bottom row also of some keyboard, very close to the CTRL key on both side of the keyboard. It enables many editing functions to be accomplished by using some keystroke combinations on the keyboard.

Shift Key: This adds to the roles of function keys. In addition, it enables the use of alternative function of a particular button (key), especially, those with more than one function on a key. E.g. use of capital letters, symbols, and numbers.

1.3. Selecting/Highlighting With Keyboard.

This is a highlighting method or style where data is selected using the computer keyboard instead of a computer mouse.

To do this:

- Move your cursor to the text or object you want to highlight, make sure that area is active,
- Hold down the shift key with one finger,
- Then use another finger to move the arrow key that points to the direction you want to highlight.

1.4 The Operating Modes Of The Keyboard.

Just like the computer mouse, keyboard has two operating modes. The two modes are Text Entering Mode and Command Mode.

a. **Text Entering Mode:** this mode gives the operator/user the opportunity to type text.
b. **Command Mode:** this is used to command the operating system/software/application to execute commands in certain ways.

2. Ways To Improve In Your Typing Skill.

1. Put Your Eyes Off The Keyboard.

This is the aspect of keyboard usage that many don't find funny because they always ask. "How can I put my eyes off the keyboard when I am running away from the occurrence of errors on my file?" My aim is to be fast, is this not going to slow me down?

Of course, there will be errors and at the same time your speed will slow down but the motive behind the introduction to this method is to make you faster than you are. Looking at your keyboard while you type can make you get a sore neck, it is better you learn to touch type because the more you type with your eyes fixed on

the screen instead of the keyboard, the faster you become.
An alternative to keeping your eyes off your keyboard is to use the *"Das Keyboard Ultimate"*.

2. Errors Challenge You

It is better to fail than to not try at all. Not trying at all is an attribute of the weak and lazybones. When you make mistakes, try again because errors are opportunities for improvement.

3. Good Posture (Position Yourself Well).

Do not adopt an awkward position while typing. You should get everything on your desk organized or arranged before sitting to type. Your posture while typing contributes to your speed and productivity.

4. Practice

Here is the conclusion of everything said above. You have to practice your shortcuts constantly. The practice alone is a way of improvement. "Practice brings improvement". Practice always.

2.1 Software That Will Help You Improve Your Typing Skill.

There are several Software programs for typing that both kids and adults can use for their typing skill. Here is a list of software that can help you improve in your typing: Mavis Beacon, Typing Instructor, Mucky Typing Adventure, Rapid Tying Tutor, Letter Chase Tying Tutor, Alice Touch Typing Tutor and many more. Personally, I love Mavis Beacon.

To learn typing using MAVIS BEACON, install Mavis Beacon software to your computer, start with keyboard lesson, then move to games. Games like *Penguin Crossing, Creature Lab*, or *Space Junk* will help you become a professional in typing. Typing and keyboard shortcuts work hand-in-hand.

Sketch of a computer mouse

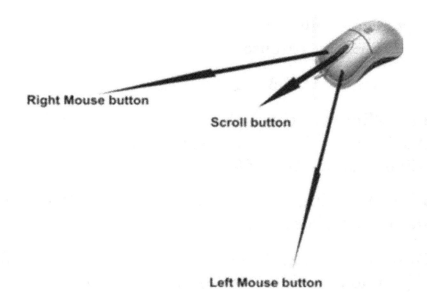

Right Mouse button

Scroll button

Left Mouse button

3. Mouse:

This is an oval-shaped portable input device with three buttons for scrolling, left clicking, and right clicking that enables work to be done effectively on a computer. The plural form of mouse is mice.

3.1 Types of Computer Mouse

- Mechanical Mouse.
- Optical Mechanical Mouse (Optomechanical).
- Laser Mouse.

- Optical Mouse.
- BlueTrack Mouse.

3.2 Forms of Clicking:

Left Clicking: This is the process of clicking the left side button of the mouse. It can also be called *clicking* without the addition of *left*.

Right Clicking: It is the process of clicking the right side button of a computer mouse.

Double Clicking: It is the process of clicking the left side button two times (twice) and immediately.

Triple Clicking: It is the process of clicking the left side button three times (thrice) and immediately.

Double clicking is used to select a word while triple clicking is used to select a sentence or paragraph.

Scroll Button: It is the little key attached to the mouse that looks like a tiny wheel. It takes you up and down a page when moved.

3.3 Mouse Pad: This is a small soft mat that is placed under the mouse to make it have a free movement.

3.4 Laptop Mouse Touchpad

This unlike the mouse we explained above is not external, rather it is inbuilt (comes with the laptop computer). With the presence of a laptop mouse touchpad, an external mouse is not needed to use a laptop, except in a case where it is malfunctioning or the operator prefers to use external one for some reasons.

The laptop mouse touchpad is usually positioned at the end of the keyboard section of a laptop computer. It is rectangular in shape with two buttons positioned below it. The two buttons/keys are used for left and right clicking just like the external mouse. Some laptops come with four mouse keys. Two placed above the mouse for left and right clicking and two other keys placed below it for the same function.

4. Definition Of Keyboard Shortcuts.

Keyboard shortcuts are defined as a series of keys, most times with combination that execute tasks which typically involve the use of mouse or other input devices.

5. Why You Should Use Shortcuts.

1. One may not be able to use a computer mouse easily because of disability or pain.

2. One may not be able to see the mouse pointer as a result of vision impairment, in such case what will the person do? The answer is SHORTCUT.

3. Research has made it known that Extensive mouse usage is related to Repetitive Syndrome Injury (RSI) greatly than the use of keyboard.

4. Keyboard shortcuts speed up computer users, making learning them a worthwhile effort.

5. When performing a job that requires precision, it is wise that you use the keyboard instead of mouse, for instance, if you are dealing with Text Editing, it is better you handle it using keyboard shortcuts than spending more time doing it with your computer mouse alone.

6. Studies calculate that using keyboard shortcuts allows working 10 times faster than working with the mouse. The time you spend looking for the mouse and then getting the cursor to the position you want is lost! Reducing your work duration by 10 times gives you greater results.

5.1 Ways To Become A Lover Of Shortcuts.

1. Always have the urge to learn new shortcut keys associated with the programs you use.
2. Be happy whenever you learn a new shortcut.

3. Try as much as you can to apply the new shortcuts you learnt.
4. Always bear it in mind that learning new shortcuts is worth it.
5. Always remember that the use of keyboard shortcuts keeps people healthy while performing computer activities.

5.2 How To Learn New Shortcut Keys

1. Do a research on them: quick references (a cheat sheet comprehensively compiled like ours) can go a long way to help you improve.
2. Buy applications that show you keyboard shortcuts every time you execute an action with mouse.
3. Disconnect your mouse if you must learn this fast.
4. Read user manuals and help topics (Whether offline or online).

5.3 Your Reward For Knowing Shortcut Keys.

1. You will get faster unimaginably.
2. Your level of efficiency will increase.
3. You will find it easy to use.
4. Opportunities are high that you will become an expert in what you do.
5. You won't have to go for **Office button**, click **New,** click **Blank and Recent**, and click **Create**

just to insert a fresh/blank page. **Ctrl +N** takes care of that in a second.

A Funny Note: Keyboarding and Mousing are in a marital union with Keyboarding being the head, so it will be unfair for anybody to put asunder between them.

5.4 Why We Emphasize On The Use of Shortcuts.

You may never leave your mouse completely unless you are ready to make your brain a box of keyboard shortcuts which will really be frustrating, just imagine yourself learning all shortcuts that go with the programs you use and their various versions. You shouldn't learn keyboard shortcuts that way.

Why we are emphasizing on the use of shortcuts is because mouse usage is becoming unusually common and unhealthy, too. So we just want to make sure both are combined so you can get fast, productive and healthy in your computer activities. All you need to know is just the most important ones associated with the programs you use.

CHAPTER 2.

15 (Fifteen) Special Keyboard Shortcuts.

The fifteen special keyboard shortcuts are fifteen (15) shortcuts every computer user should know.

The following is a list of keyboard shortcuts every computer user should know:

1. **Ctrl + A:** Control A, highlights or selects everything you have in the environment where you are working.

    *If you are like **"Wow, the content of this document is large and there is no time to select all of it, besides, it's going to mount pressure on my computer?"** Using the mouse for this is an outdated method of handling a task like selecting all, Ctrl+A will take care of that in a second.*

15

2. **Ctrl + C:** Control C copies any highlighted or selected element within the work environment.
    Saves the time and stress which would have been used to right click and click again just to copy. Use ctrl+c.

3. **Ctrl + N:** Control N opens a new window or file.
    Instead of clicking **File, New, blank/ template** *and another* **click**, *just press* **Ctrl + N** *and a fresh page or window will appear instantly.*

4. **Ctrl + O:** Control O opens a new program.
    Use ctrl +O when you want to locate / open a file or program.

5. **Ctrl + P:** Control P prints the active document.
    Always use this to locate the printer dialog box, and thereafter print.

6. **Ctrl + S:** Control S saves a new document or file and changes made by the user.
    Please stop! Don't use the mouse. Just press Ctrl+S and everything will be saved.

7. **Ctrl +V:** Control V pastes copied elements into the active area of the program in use.

Using ctrl+V in a case like this Saves the time and stress of right clicking and clicking again just to paste.

8. **Ctrl + W:** Control W is used to close the page you are working on when you want to leave the work environment.

    "There is a way Debby does this without using the mouse. Oh my God, why didn't I learn it then?" Don't worry, I have the answer. Debby presses Ctrl+W to close active windows.

9. **Ctrl + X:** Control X cuts elements (making the elements to disappear from their original place). The difference between cutting and deleting elements is that in Cutting, what was cut doesn't get lost permanently but prepares itself so that it can be pasted on another location defined by the user.

    *Use ctrl+x when you think **"this shouldn't be here and I can't stand the stress of retyping or redesigning it on the rightful place it belongs".***

10. **Ctrl + Y:** Control Y undoes already done actions.

    Ctrl+Z brought back what you didn't need? Press Ctrl+ Y to remove it again.

11. **Ctrl + Z:** Control Z redoes actions. *Can't find what you typed now or a picture you inserted, it suddenly disappeared or you mistakenly removed it? Press Ctrl+Z to bring it back.*

12. **Alt + F4:** Alternative F4 closes active windows or items.

    *You don't need to move the mouse in order to close an active window, just press **Alt + F4**. Also use it when you are done or you don't want somebody who is coming to see what you are doing.*

13. **Ctrl + F6:** Control F6 Navigates between open windows, making it possible for a user to see what is happening in windows that are active. *Are you working in Microsoft Word and want to find out if the other active window where your browser is loading a page is still progressing?* Use Ctrl + F6.

14. **F1:** This displays the help window.

    *Is your computer malfunctioning? Use **F1** to find help when you don't know what next to do.*

15. **F12:** This enables user to make changes to an already saved document.

    F12 is the shortcut to use when you want to change the format in which you saved your existing document, password it, change its name, change the file location or destination, or make other changes to it. It will save you time.

Note: The Control (Ctrl) key on Windows and Linux operating system is the same thing as Command (Cmmd) key on a Macintosh computer. So if you replace Control with Command key on a Mac computer for the special shortcuts listed above, you will get the same result.

CHAPTER 3.

Keyboard Shortcuts for use in Adobe Premiere Pro CC.

About the program: This is a timeline video editing software application used by videographers to edit, manipulate, and export their video works.

A fresh topic ⌐⌐➤

Visual Keyboard Layout for Assigning Keyboard Shortcuts.

You can use the keyboard GUI to see which keys have been assigned and which are available for assignment. A tool tip reveals the full command name when you hover over a key in the Keyboard layout. When you select a modifier key on the keyboard layout, the keyboard displays all the shortcuts which require that modifier. You can also press the modifier key on the hardware keyboard to achieve this result.

When you select a key on the Keyboard Layout, you can view all the commands that are assigned to that unmodified key and all other modifier combinations.

- Premiere Pro detects the keyboard hardware and the appropriate keyboard layout is displayed accordingly.
- When Premiere Pro detects a non-supported keyboard, the default view is to display the U.S. English keyboard. By default, the Adobe Premiere Pro Default preset is displayed.
- When you change a shortcut, the preset pop-up menu gets changed to Custom. After you make the required changes, you can choose Save As to save the customized shortcut set as a preset.

Color coding

- Keys shaded in purple are application-wide shortcuts.
- Keys shaded in green are panel-specific shortcuts.
- Keys shaded in both purple and green represent the panel commands that have been assigned to keys that also have an application command already assigned to them.

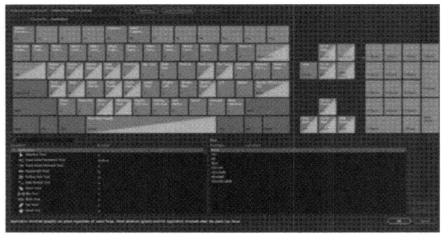

Application shortcuts

Application shortcuts and panel shortcuts

- Commands can be assigned for application shortcuts and command shortcuts.
- Application shortcuts function regardless of panel focus (with some exceptions) and panel shortcuts function only when the panel is in focus.
- Certain keyboard shortcuts work only in specific panels. This means that you can have more than once shortcut assigned to the same key. You can also make use of the pop-up window that shows only a certain batch of panel shortcuts (for example, only for the timeline).
- When a Panel Shortcut has the same assigned shortcut as an application Shortcut, the

application shortcut does not function when that panel has focus.

- You can search for commands in the Command List, which is filtered by the search criteria. You can also assign shortcuts by clicking in the shortcut column and tapping keys on their keyboard to create the shortcut (including adding modifiers).

A warning indicating a shortcut conflict appears when:

1. An application shortcut already in use by another application shortcut.
2. A panel shortcut is already in use by another command in the same panel.
3. A panel shortcut overrides an application shortcut when that panel has focus.

You can also click drag to assign commands to keys on the keyboard layout or the Key modifier list.

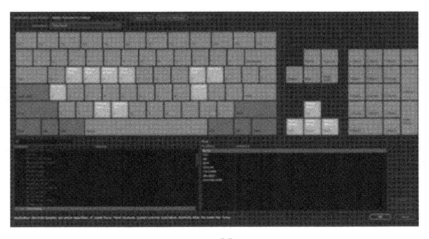

Panel shortcuts

Shortcut assignment using Drag-and-Drop

You can also assign shortcuts by dragging a command from the command List onto a key in the Keyboard Layout, or onto a modifier combination for the currently selected key displayed in the Key Modifier List. To assign a command to a key along with a modifier, hold down the modifiers during drag-and-drop.

Conflict resolution

When there is a conflict with a shortcut that is already in use with another command:

- A warning appears at the bottom of the editor
- Undo and Clear buttons in the lower right corner are enabled.
- The command in conflict is highlighted in blue, and clicking this automatically selects the command in the command list.
- This allows users to easily change the assignment for the conflicting command.

Note:

Use this instead of the 'Go To' button used in former releases.

End of Topic.

A fresh topic ⌐↳

Default Keyboard Shortcuts in Adobe Premiere Pro CC.

Many commands have keyboard shortcut equivalents, so you can complete tasks with minimal use of the mouse. You can also create or edit keyboard shortcuts.

Now use the following list of keyboard shortcuts to enhance your productivity in Adobe Premiere Pro.

File.

Results	Windows Shortcut	Mac OS Shortcut
Project/Production...	Ctrl+Alt+N	Opt+Cmd+N
Sequence...	Ctrl+N	Cmd+N
Bin		Cmd+/
Title...	Ctrl+T	Cmd+T
Open Project/Production...	Ctrl+O	Cmd+O
Browse in Adobe Bridge...	Ctrl+Alt+O	Opt+Cmd+O
Close Project	Ctrl+Shift+W	Shift+Cmd+W

Close	Ctrl+W	Cmd+W
Save	Ctrl+S	Cmd+S
Save As...	Ctrl+Shift+S	Shift+Cmd+S
Save a Copy...	Ctrl+Alt+S	Opt+Cmd+S
Capture...	F5	F5
Batch Capture...	F6	F6
Import from Media Browser	Ctrl+Alt+I	Opt+Cmd+I
Import...	Ctrl+I	Cmd+I
Export Media...	Ctrl+M	Cmd+M
Get Properties for Selection...	Ctrl+Shift+H	Shift+Cmd+H
Exit	Ctrl+Q	

Edit.

Results	Windows Shortcut	Mac OS Shortcut
Undo	Ctrl+Z	Cmd+Z
Redo	Ctrl+Shift+Z	Shift+Cmd+Z
Cut	Ctrl+X	Cmd+X
Copy	Ctrl+C	Cmd+C
Paste	Ctrl+V	Cmd+V
Paste Insert	Ctrl+Shift+V	Shift+Cmd+V
Paste Attributes	Ctrl+Alt+V	Opt+Cmd+V
Clear	Delete	Forward Delete

Ripple Delete	Shift+Delete	Shift+Forward Delete
Duplicate	Ctrl+Shift+/	Shift+Cmd+/
Select All	Ctrl+A	Cmd+A
Deselect All	Ctrl+Shift+A	Shift+Cmd+A
Find...	Ctrl+F	Cmd+F
Edit Original	Ctrl+E	Cmd+E
Keyboard Shortcuts	Ctrl+Alt+K	Cmd+Opt+K

Clip.

Results	Windows Shortcut	Mac OS Shortcut
Make Subclip...		Cmd+U
Audio Channels...		Shift+G
Speed/Duration...	Ctrl+R	Cmd+R
Insert	,	,
Overwrite	.	.
Enable		Shift+Cmd+E
Link		Cmd+l
Group	Ctrl+G	Cmd+G
Ungroup	Ctrl+Shift+G	Shift+Cmd+G

Sequence.

Results	Windows Shortcut	Mac OS Shortcut

Render Effects in Work Area/In to Out	Enter	Return
Match Frame	F	F
Reverse Match Frame	Shift+R	Shift+R
Add Edit	Ctrl+K	Cmd+K
Add Edit to All Tracks	Ctrl+Shift+K	Shift+Cmd+K
Trim Edit	T	T
Extend Selected Edit to Playhead	E	E
Apply Video Transition	Ctrl+D	Cmd+D
Apply Audio Transition	Ctrl+Shift+D	Shift+Cmd+D
Apply Default Transitions to Selection		Shift+D
Lift	;	;
Extract	'	'
Zoom In	=	=
Zoom Out	-	-
Go to Gap		
Next in Sequence		Shift+;
Previous in Sequence		Opt+;
Snap	S	S

Marker.

Results	Windows Shortcut	Mac OS Shortcut
Mark In	I	I
Mark Out	O	O
Mark Clip	X	X
Mark Selection	/	/
Go to In	Shift+I	Shift+I
Go to Out	Shift+O	Shift+O
Clear In	Ctrl+Shift+I	Opt+I
Clear Out	Ctrl+Shift+O	Opt+O
Clear In and Out	Ctrl+Shift+X	Opt+X
Add Marker	M	M
Go to Next Marker	Shift+M	Shift+M
Go to Previous Marker	Ctrl+Shift+M	Shift+Cmd+M
Clear Current Marker	Ctrl+Alt+M	Opt+M
Clear All Markers	Ctrl+Alt+Shift+M	Opt+Cmd+M
Type Alignment		
Left	Ctrl+Shift+L	Shift+Cmd+L
Center	Ctrl+Shift+C	Shift+Cmd+C
Right	Ctrl+Shift+R	Shift+Cmd+R

Tab Stops...	Ctrl+Shift+T	Shift+Cmd+T
Templates...	Ctrl+J	Cmd+J
Select		
Next Object Above	Ctrl+Alt+]	Opt+Cmd+]
Next Object Below	Ctrl+Alt+[	Opt+Cmd+[
Arrange		
Bring to Front	Ctrl+Shift+]	Shift+Cmd+]
Bring Forward	Ctrl+]	Cmd+]
Send to Back	Ctrl+Shift+[	Shift+Cmd+[
Send Backward	Ctrl+[	Cmd+[

Window.

Workspace

Results	Windows Shortcut	Mac OS Shortcut
Reset Current Workspace...		Opt+Shift +0
Audio Clip Mixer	Shift+9	Shift+9
Audio Track Mixer	Shift+6	Shift+6
Effect Controls	Shift+5	Shift+5
Effects	Shift+7	Shift+7
Media Browser	Shift+8	Shift+8

Program Monitor	Shift+4	Shift+4
Project	Shift+1	Shift+1
Source Monitor	Shift+2	Shift+2
Timelines	Shift+3	Shift+3
Show/hide application title	Ctrl+	Cmd+

Help.

Results	Windows Shortcut	Mac OS Shortcut
Adobe Premiere Pro Help...	F1	F1
Clear Poster Frame	Cmd+Shift+P	Opt+P
Cut to Camera 1	Cmd+1	Ctrl+1
Cut to Camera 2	Cmd+2	Ctrl+2
Cut to Camera 3	Cmd+3	Ctrl+3
Cut to Camera 4	Cmd+4	Ctrl+4
Cut to Camera 5	Cmd+5	Ctrl+5
Cut to Camera 6	Cmd+6	Ctrl+6
Cut to Camera 7	Cmd+7	Ctrl+7
Cut to Camera 8	Cmd+8	Ctrl+8
Cut to Camera 9	Cmd+9	Ctrl+9
Decrease Clip Volume		[

		Shift+[
Decrease Clip Volume Many		Shift+[
Expand All Tracks		Shift+=
Export Frame	Ctrl+Shift+E	Shift+E
Extend Next Edit To Playhead		Shift+W
Extend Previous Edit To Playhead		Shift+Q

Panels.

Audio Mixer Panel Menu

Results	Windows Shortcut	Mac OS Shortcut
Show/Hide Tracks...	Ctrl+Alt+T	Opt+Cmd+T
Loop		Cmd+L
Meter Input Only	Ctrl+Shift+I	Ctrl+Shift+I
Capture Panel		
Record Video	V	V
Record Audio	A	A
Eject	E	E
Fast Forward	F	F
Go to In point	Q	Q
Go to Out point	W	W

Record	G	G
Rewind	R	R
Step Back	Left	Left
Step Forward	Right	Right
Stop	S	S
Effect Controls Panel Menu		
Remove Selected Effect	Backspace	Delete
Effects Panel Menu		
New Custom Bin	Ctrl+/	Cmd+/
Delete Custom Item	Backspace	Delete
History Panel Menu		
Step Backward	Left	Left
Step Forward	Right	Right
Delete	Backspace	Delete
Open in Source Monitor	Shift+O	Shift+O
Parent Directory	Ctrl+Up	Cmd+Up
Select Directory List		Shift+Left
Select Media List		Shift+Right
Loop		Cmd+L
Play	Space	Space
Go to Next Edit Point	Down	Down

Go to Previous Edit Point	Up	Up
Play/Stop Toggle	Space	Space
Record On/Off Toggle	o	o
Step Back	Left	Left
Step Forward	Right	Right
Loop		Cmd+L

Tools.

Results	Windows Shortcut	Mac OS Shortcut
Selection Tool	V	V
Track Select Tool	A	A
Ripple Edit Tool	B	B
Rolling Edit Tool	N	N
Rate Stretch Tool	R	R
Razor Tool	C	C
Slip Tool	Y	Y
Slide Tool	U	U
Pen Tool	P	P
Hand Tool	H	H
Zoom Tool	Z	Z

Multi-camera.

Result	Windows Shortcut	Mac OS Shortcut
Go to Next Edit Point	Down	Down
Go to Next Edit Point on Any Track	Shift+Down	Shift+Down
Go to Previous Edit Point	Up	Up
Go to Previous Edit Point on Any Track	Shift+Up	Shift+Up
Go to Selected Clip End	Shift+End	Shift+End
Go to Selected Clip Start	Shift+Home	Shift+Home
Go to Sequence-Clip End	End	End
Go to Sequence-Clip Start	Home	Home
Increase Clip Volume	]	]
Increase Clip Volume Many	Shift+]	Shift+]

Maximize or Restore Active Frame	Shift+`	Shift+`
Maximize or Restore Frame Under Cursor	`	`
Minimize All Tracks	Shift+-	Shift+-
Play Around	Shift+K	Shift+K
Play In to Out	Ctrl+Shift+Space	Opt+K
Play In to Out with Preroll/Postroll	Shift+Space	Shift+Space
Play from Playhead to Out Point	Ctrl+Space	Ctrl+Space
Play-Stop Toggle	Space	SpaceRecord Voiceover
Reveal Nested Sequence	Ctrl+Shift+F	Shift+T
Ripple Trim Next Edit To Playhead	W	W
Ripple Trim Previous Edit To Playhead	Q	Q
Select Camera 1	1	1

Select Camera 2	2	2
Select Camera 3	3	3
Select Camera 4	4	4
Select Camera 5	5	5
Select Camera 6	6	6
Select Camera 7	7	7
Select Camera 8	8	8
Select Camera 9	9	9
Select Find Box	Shift+F	Shift+F
Select Clip at Playhead	D	D
Select Next Clip	Ctrl+Down	Cmd+Down
Select Next Panel	Ctrl+Shift+.	Ctrl+Shift+.
Select Previous Clip	Ctrl+Up	Cmd+Up
Select Previous Panel	Ctrl+Shift+,	Ctrl+Shift+,
Set Poster Frame	Shift+P	Cmd+P
Shuttle Left	J	J

Shuttle Right	L	L
Shuttle Slow Left	Shift+J	Shift+J
Shuttle Slow Right	Shift+L	Shift+L
Shuttle Stop	K	K
Step Back	Left	Left
Step Back Five Frames - Units	Shift+Left	Shift+Left
Step Forward	Right	Right
Step Forward Five Frames - Units	Shift+Right	Shift+Right
Toggle All Audio Targets	Ctrl+9	Cmd+9
Toggle All Source Audio	Ctrl+Alt+9	Opt+Cmd+9
Toggle All Source Video	Ctrl+Alt+0	Opt+Cmd+0
Toggle All Video Targets	Ctrl+0	Cmd+0
Toggle Audio During Scrubbing	Shift+S	Shift+S
Toggle Control Surface Clip Mixer Mode		
Toggle Full Screen	Ctrl+`	Ctrl+`

Toggle Multi-Camera View	Shift+0	Shift+0
Toggle Trim Type	Shift+T	Ctrl+T
Trim Backward	Ctrl+Left	Opt+Left
Trim Backward Many	Ctrl+Shift+Left	Opt+Shift+Left
Trim Forward	Ctrl+Right	Opt+Right
Trim Forward Many	Ctrl+Shift+Right	Opt+Shift+Right
Trim Next Edit to Playhead	Ctrl+Alt+W	Opt+W
Trim Previous Edit to Playhead	Ctrl+Alt+Q	Opt+Q

Project Panel.

Result	Windows Shortcut	Mac OS Shortcut
Workspace 1	Alt+Shift+1	Opt+Shift+1
Workspace 2	Alt+Shift+2	Opt+Shift+2
Workspace 3	Alt+Shift+3	Opt+Shift+3
Workspace 4	Alt+Shift+4	Opt+Shift+4
Workspace 5	Alt+Shift+5	Opt+Shift+5
Workspace 6	Alt+Shift+6	Opt+Shift+6
Workspace 7	Alt+Shift+7	Opt+Shift+7

Workspace 8	Alt+Shift+8	Opt+Shift+8
Workspace 9	Alt+Shift+9	Opt+Shift+9
Zoom to Sequence	\	\
Extend Selection Up	Shift+Up	Shift+Up
Move Selection Down	Down	Down
Move Selection End	End	End
Move Selection Home	Home	Home
Move Selection Left	Left	Left
Move Selection Page Down	Page Down	Page Down
Move Selection Page Up	Page Up	Page Up
Move Selection Right	Right	Right
Move Selection Up	Up	Up
Next Column Field	Tab	Tab
Next Row Field	Enter	Return
Open in Source Monitor	Shift+O	Shift+O
Previous Column Field	Shift+Tab	Shift+Tab
Previous Row Field	Shift+Enter	Shift+Return

Thumbnail Size Next	Shift+]	Shift+]
Thumbnail Size Previous	Shift+[	Shift+[
Toggle View	Shift+\	Shift+\

Timeline Panel.

Result	Windows Shortcut	Mac OS Shortcut
Add Clip Marker	Ctrl+1	
Clear Selection	Backspace	Delete
Decrease Audio Tracks Height	Alt+-	Opt+-
Decrease Video Tracks Height	Ctrl+-	Cmd+-
Increase Audio Tracks Height	Alt+=	Opt+=
Increase Video Tracks Height	Ctrl+=	Cmd+=

Nudge Clip Selection Left Five Frames	Alt+Shift+Left	Shift+Cmd+Left
Nudge Clip Selection Left One Frame	Alt+Left	Cmd+Left
Nudge Clip Selection Right Five Frames	Alt+Shift+Right	Shift+Cmd+Right
Nudge Clip Selection Right One Frame	Alt+Right	Cmd+Right
Ripple Delete	Alt+Backspace	Opt+Delete
Set Work Area Bar In Point	Alt+[	Opt+[
Set Work Area Bar Out Point	Alt+]	Opt+]

Show Next Screen	Page Down	Page Down
Show Previous Screen	Page Up	Page Up
Slide Clip Selection Left Five Frames	Alt+Shift+,	Opt+Shift+,
Slide Clip Selection Left One Frame	Alt+,	Opt+,
Slide Clip Selection Right Five Frames	Alt+Shift+.	Opt+Shift+.
Slide Clip Selection Right One Frame	Alt+.	Opt+.
Slip Clip Selection Left Five Frames	Ctrl+Alt+Shift+Left	Opt+Shift+Cmd+Left

Slip Clip Selection Left One Frame	Ctrl+Alt+Left	Opt+Cmd+Left
Slip Clip Selection Right Five Frames	Ctrl+Alt+Shift+Right	Opt+Shift+Cmd+Right
Slip Clip Selection Right One Frame	Ctrl+Alt+Right	Opt+Cmd+Right

Titler.

Result	Windows Shortcut	Mac OS Shortcut
Arc Tool	A	A
Bold	Ctrl+B	Cmd+B
Decrease Kerning by Five Units	Alt+Shift+Left	Opt+Shift+Left
Decrease Kerning by One Unit	Alt+Left	Opt+Left

Decrease Leading by Five Units	Alt+Shift+Down	Opt+Shift+Down
Decrease Leading by One Unit	Alt+Down	Opt+Down
Decrease Text Size by Five Points	Ctrl+Alt+Shift+Left	Opt+Shift+Cmd+Left
Decrease Text Size by One Point	Ctrl+Alt+Left	Opt+Cmd+Left
Ellipse Tool	E	E
Increase Kerning by Five Units	Alt+Shift+Right	Opt+Shift+Right
Increase Kerning by One Unit	Alt+Right	Opt+Right
Increase Leading by Five Units	Alt+Shift+Up	Opt+Shift+Up
Increase Leading by One Unit	Alt+Up	Opt+Up

Increase Text Size by Five Points	Ctrl+Alt+Shift+Right	Opt+Shift+Cmd+Right
Increase Text Size by One Point	Ctrl+Alt+Right	Opt+Cmd+Right
Insert Copyright Symbol	Ctrl+Alt+Shift+C	Opt+Shift+Cmd+C
Insert Registered Symbol	Ctrl+Alt+Shift+R	Opt+Shift+Cmd+R
Italic	Ctrl+I	Cmd+I
Line Tool	L	L
Nudge Selected Object Down by Five Pixels	Shift+Down	Shift+Down
Nudge Selected Object Down by One Pixel	Down	Down
Nudge Selected Object Left	Shift+Left	Shift+Left

by Five Pixels		
Nudge Selected Object Left by One Pixel	Left	Left
Nudge Selected Object Right by Five Pixels	Shift+Right	Shift+Right
Nudge Selected Object Right by One Pixel	Right	Right
Nudge Selected Object Up by Five Pixels	Shift+Up	Shift+Up
Nudge Selected Object Up by One Pixel	Up	Up
Path Type Tool		
Pen Tool	P	P

Position Objects to Bottom Title Safe Margin	Ctrl+Shift+D	Shift+Cmd+D
Position Objects to Left Title Safe Margin	Ctrl+Shift+F	Shift+Cmd+F
Position Objects to Top Title Safe Margin	Ctrl+Shift+O	Shift+Cmd+O
Rectangle Tool	R	R
Rotation Tool	O	O
Selection Tool	V	V
Type Tool	T	T
Underline	Ctrl+U	Cmd+U
Vertical Type Tool	C	C
Wedge Tool	W	W

Trim Monitor Panel.

Result	Windows Shortcut	Mac OS Shortcut
Focus Both Outgoing and Incoming	Alt+1	Opt+1
Focus on Incoming Side	Alt+3	Opt+3
Focus on Outgoing Side	Alt+2	Opt+2
Loop	Ctrl+L	Cmd+L
Trim Backward by Large Trim Offset	Alt+Shift+Left	Opt+Shift+Left
Trim Backward by One Frame	Alt+Left	Opt+Left
Trim Forward by Large Trim Offset	Alt+Shift+Right	Opt+Shift+Right
Trim Forward by One Frame	Alt+Right	Opt+Right

End of Topic.

A fresh topic ⌐⌐→

Finding Keyboard Shortcuts.

Find the keyboard shortcuts for a tool, button, or menu command by doing any of the following:

- For a tool or button, hold the pointer over the tool or button until its tool tip appears. If available, the keyboard shortcut appears in the tool tip after the tool description.
- For menu commands, look for the keyboard shortcut at the right of the command.
- For the most-used keyboard shortcuts not shown in tool tips or on menus, see the tables in this article. For a complete list of default and current shortcuts, choose Edit > Keyboard Shortcuts (Windows) or Premiere Pro > Keyboard Shortcuts (Mac OS)
- Use the search field in the Keyboard Customization dialog box to find specific commands quickly.

Customize or Load Keyboard Shortcuts.

You can set shortcuts to match shortcuts in other software you use. If other sets are available, you can choose them from the Set menu in the Keyboard Customization dialog box.

1. For customizing keyboard shortcuts, choose one of the following:
   o In Windows, choose Edit > Keyboard Shortcuts
   o In Mac OS, choose Premiere Pro > Keyboard Shortcuts
2. In the Keyboard Customization dialog box, choose an option from the menu:

Application

Displays commands found in the menu bar, organized by category.

Panels

Displays commands associated with panels and menus.

Tools

Displays a list of tool icons.

3. In the Command column, view the command for which you want to create or change a shortcut. If necessary, click the triangle next to the name of a category to reveal the commands it includes.
4. Click in the item's shortcut field to select it.
5. Type the shortcut you want to use for the item. The Keyboard Customization dialog box displays an alert if the shortcut you choose is already in use.

6. Do one of the following:
    o To erase a shortcut and return it to the command that originally had it, click Undo.
    o To jump to the command that previously had the shortcut, click Go To.
    o To simply delete the shortcut you typed, click Clear.
    o To reenter the shortcut you typed previously, click Redo.
7. Repeat the procedure to enter as many shortcuts as you want. When you're finished, click Save As, type a name for your Key Set, and click Save.

Note:

The operating system reserves some commands. You cannot reassign those commands to Premiere Pro. Also, you cannot assign the plus (+) and minus (-) keys on the numeric keypad because they are necessary for entering relative timecode values. You can assign the minus (−) key on the main keyboard, however.

Copy keyboard shortcuts from one computer to another.

Sync keyboard shortcuts using Creative Cloud

Premiere Pro CC lets you quickly and easily sync keyboard shortcuts between computers using the Sync

Settings feature. Using Sync Settings, you can upload the customized keyboard shortcuts from your computer to Creative Cloud. Then, you can sync the keyboard shortcuts from Creative Cloud to any other computer.

Note:

Keyboard shortcuts are synchronized for the same platform only, and not between Windows and Mac OS platforms. That is, keyboard shortcuts created for Windows only sync with a Windows computer. Mac OS keyboard shortcuts only sync with a Mac OS computer.

Manually copy keyboard shortcuts

You can copy your customized keyboard shortcuts from one computer to another computer, or to another location on your computer.

1. Locate the keyboard shortcuts (.kys) file that you want to copy to another computer.

   The location of the customized keyboard shortcuts file depends on whether you've signed in to Creative Cloud Sync Settings in Premiere Pro CC or not.

   Signed into Creative Cloud Sync Settings

   ○ Win: Users\[user name]\Documents\Adobe\Premiere

Pro\[version]\Profile-CreativeCloud-\Win\

- o Mac: Users/[user name]/Documents/Adobe/Premiere Pro/[version]/Profile-CreativeCloud-/Mac/

Signed out of Creative Cloud Sync Settings

- o Win: Users\[user name]\Documents\Adobe\Premiere Pro\[version]\Profile-username\Win\
- o Mac: Users/[user name]/Documents/Adobe/Premiere Pro/[version]/Profile-username/Mac/

Note:

[version] can be 7.0 or 8.0

2. Copy the keyboard shortcuts (.kys) file and paste into the required file location.

To copy the keyboard shortcuts file to a location on a different computer, copy the .kys file to a removable drive, like a USB thumb drive. Then, copy the .kys file from the removable drive to the appropriate location in the new computer.

Assign multiple keyboard shortcuts to a command.

You can assign multiple keyboard shortcuts for a single command.

The Keyboard Shortcuts dialog displays the keyboard shortcut as an editable button, which lets you change, add multiple shortcuts, or delete shortcuts.

Add more shortcuts

To add more shortcuts to a command, click to the right of an existing shortcut. If there is no existing shortcut, click anywhere in the Shortcut column. A new shortcut button is created in which you can type the shortcut.

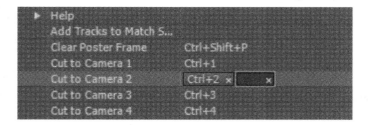

Edit a shortcut

To edit a shortcut, click the shortcut text in the Shortcuts column. The text is replaced with an editable button. Type the shortcut that you want to use. If the shortcut you type is already in use, an alert appears.

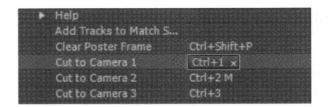

Delete a shortcut

To delete a shortcut, click '**x**' in the editable shortcut button.

Remove Shortcuts

1. Do one of the following:
   - In Windows, choose Edit > Keyboard Shortcuts
   - In Mac OS, choose Premiere Pro > Keyboard Shortcuts
2. Do one of the following:
   - To remove a shortcut, select the shortcut you want to remove, and click Clear.
   - To remove a set of shortcuts, choose the key set from the Set menu and click Delete. When prompted in the warning dialog box, click Delete to confirm your choice.

Applies to: *Adobe Premiere Pro CC.*

Customer's Page.

This page is for customers who enjoyed Adobe Premiere Pro CC Keyboard Shortcuts.

Our beloved and respectable reader, we thank you very much for your patronage. Please we will appreciate it more if you rate and review this book; that is if it was helpful to you. Thank you.

Download Our EBooks Today For Free.

In order to appreciate our customers, we have made some of our titles available at 0.00. They are totally free. Feel free to get a copy of the free titles.

Here are books we give to our customers free of charge:

(A) For Keyboard Shortcuts in Windows check:

Windows 7 Keyboard Shortcuts.

(B) For Keyboard Shortcuts in Office 2016 for Windows check:

Word 2016 Keyboard Shortcuts For Windows.

(C) For Keyboard Shortcuts in Office 2016 for Mac check:

OneNote 2016 Keyboard Shortcuts For Macintosh.

Follow this link to download any of the titles listed above for free.

Note: Feel free to download them from our website or your favorite bookstore today. Thank you.

Other Books By This Publisher.

Titles for single programs under Shortcut Matters Series are not part of this list.

S/N	Title	Series
Series A: Limits Breaking Quotes.		
1	Discover Your Key Christian Quotes	Limits Breaking Quotes
Series B: Shortcut Matters.		
1	Windows 7 Shortcuts	Shortcut Matters
2	Windows 7 Shortcuts & Tips	Shortcut Matters
3	Windows 8.1 Shortcuts	Shortcut Matters
4	Windows 10 Shortcut Keys	Shortcut Matters
5	Microsoft Office 2007 Keyboard Shortcuts For Windows.	Shortcut Matters
6	Microsoft Office 2010 Shortcuts For Windows.	Shortcut Matters
7	Microsoft Office 2013 Shortcuts For Windows.	Shortcut Matters
8	Microsoft Office 2016 Shortcuts For Windows.	Shortcut Matters
9	Microsoft Office 2016 Keyboard Shortcuts For Macintosh.	Shortcut Matters
10	Top 11 Adobe Programs Keyboard Shortcuts	Shortcut Matters
11	Top 10 Email Service Providers Keyboard Shortcuts	Shortcut Matters
12	Hot Corel Programs Keyboard Shortcuts	Shortcut Matters

13	Top 10 Browsers Keyboard Shortcuts	Shortcut Matters
14	Microsoft Browsers Keyboard Shortcuts.	Shortcut Matters
15	Popular Email Service Providers Keyboard Shortcuts	Shortcut Matters
16	Professional Video Editing with Keyboard Shortcuts.	Shortcut Matters
17	Popular Web Browsers Keyboard Shortcuts.	Shortcut Matters

Series C: Teach Yourself.

1	Teach Yourself Computer Fundamentals	Teach Yourself
2	Teach Yourself Computer Fundamentals Workbook	Teach Yourself

Series D: For Painless Publishing

1	Self-Publish it with CreateSpace.	For Painless Publishing
2	Where is my money? Now solved for Kindle and CreateSpace	For Painless Publishing
3	Describe it on Amazon	For Painless Publishing